A GRAPHIC GUIDE TO WRITING SMART AS HELL GOALS!

BY GLENN HUGHES

FIND US ON THE WEB AT *SMARTASHELL.COM*.

TO REPORT ERRORS, PLEASE SEND A NOTE TO INFO@SMARTASHELL.COM.

NOTICE OF RIGHTS

COPYRIGHT © 2015 BY SMART AS HELL. ALL RIGHTS RESERVED. NO PART OF THIS BOOK MAY BE REPRODUCED OR TRANSMITTED IN ANY FORM BY ANY MEANS, ELECTRONIC, MECHANICAL, PHOTOCOPYING, RECORDING, OR OTHERWISE, WITHOUT THE PRIOR WRITTEN PERMISSION OF THE PUBLISHER.

ALL IMAGES © GLENN HUGHES

ISBN: 978-0-9894655-4-0
LCCN: 2015914742
SEPT 30, 2015

FOR REPRINTS AND EXCERPTS PERMISSION, CONTACT INFO@SMARTASHELL.COM.

NOTICE OF LIABILITY

THE INFORMATION IN THIS BOOK IS DISTRIBUTED ON AN "AS IS" BASIS WITHOUT WARRANTY. WHILE EVERY PRECAUTION HAS BEEN TAKEN IN THE PREPARATION OF THE BOOK, NEITHER THE AUTHOR NOR THE PUBLISHER SHALL HAVE ANY LIABILITY TO ANY PERSON OR ENTITY WITH RESPECT TO ANY LOSS OR DAMAGE CAUSED OR ALLEGED TO BE CAUSED DIRECTLY OR INDIRECTLY BY THE INSTRUCTIONS CONTAINED IN THIS BOOK.

SAH PUBLISHING

SAN JOSE, CALIFORNIA, USA

ACKNOWLEDGMENTS

- *ANGIE ELSCHLAGER*
  FOR HER WILLINGNESS TO SAY, "THAT MAKES NO SENSE", WHEN MY IDEAS AREN'T FULLY DEVELOPED.
- *SAM HUGHES*
  FOR SHOWING ME – FROM AN EARLY AGE – WHAT 'SMART AS HELL' LOOKS LIKE.
- *ED MUZIO*
  FOR BEING THE FIRST TO SAY, "YOU SHOULD WRITE A BOOK ABOUT GOALS. I'D BUY IT!"
- *CAL WICK*
  FOR HELPING ME INTRODUCE SMART AS HELL TO A BROADER AUDIENCE.
- *NANCY DUARTE AND DAVE GRAY*
  FOR PUSHING ME TO CREATE A GRAPHIC VERSION OF MY WORK.
- *ISPI (THE INTERNATIONAL SOCIETY FOR PERFORMANCE IMPROVEMENT) AND TRAINING MAGAZINE*
  FOR INVITING ME TO SHARE MY WORK WITH THEIR COMMUNITIES.
- *CYNTHIA RIHA & DEB DEMAY*
  FOR BEING EARLY ADOPTERS OF SMART AS HELL.
- *KLA-TENCOR CORPORATION*
  FOR ENCOURAGING MY WORK IN EVERY WAY.

CONTENTS

OBJECTIVES	VII
FOREWORD BY SIVASAILAM 'THIAGI' THIAGARAJAN	IX
PART ONE: MICKEY'S BAD MORNING	1
PART TWO: MICKEY ASKS FOR HELP	7
PART THREE: GETTING S.M.A.R.T	19
PART FOUR: MICKEY MEETS THE SMARTOMETER	39
PART FIVE: MICKEY FINDS CLARITY	179
PART SIX: ALIGNING WITH AMY	193
PART SEVEN: WRAPPING IT UP	211
PART EIGHT: RESOURCES	217

FIND SUPPLEMENTAL VIDEOS, WORKSHEETS, AND LINKS AT:

HTTP://SMARTASHELL.COM/BLOG/SAHGG

OBJECTIVES

AFTER COMPLETING THIS BOOK, YOU WILL BE ABLE TO WRITE GOALS THAT DRIVE ACTION, ALIGNMENT, AND ACHIEVEMENT. SPECIFICALLY, YOU WILL:

- DEFINE THE S.M.A.R.T ACRONYM (PG. 35)
- ASSESS THE QUALITY OF A GOAL, USING THE SMARTOMETER LITE (PG. 42)
- MEASURE THE QUALITY OF YOUR DATA, USING THE DATA CONFIDENCE SCORECARD (PG. 87)
- ASSESS WHETHER A GOAL IS AGGRESSIVELY S.E.T. (PG. 103)
- PREDICT THE INTENDED AND UNINTENDED CONSEQUENCES OF A GOAL OR ACTION, USING THE RIPPLE MAP (PG. 142)
- BRAINSTORM THE INGREDIENTS OF A GOAL, USING THE SMARTSHEET (PG. 181)
- CREATE A GOAL STATEMENT USING THE SMART STORYBOARD (PG. 189)
- DEFINE 13 APPLICATIONS FOR SMART GOALS (PG. 213)
- WRITE A SMART AS HELL GOAL, USING THE SMARTSHEET, SMART STORYBOARD, AND SMARTOMETER LITE

FOREWORD

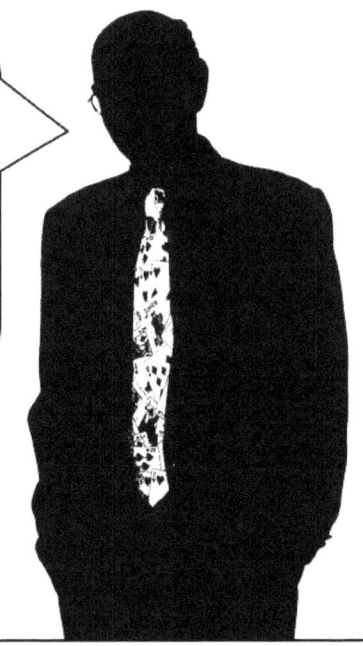

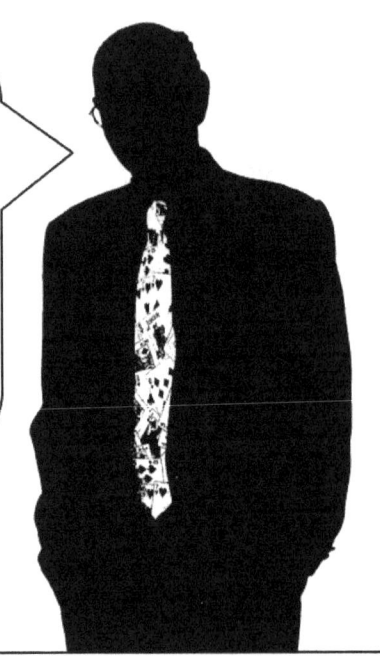

PART ONE

MICKEY'S BAD MORNING

PART TWO

MICKEY ASKS FOR HELP

PART THREE

GETTING S.M.A.R.T.

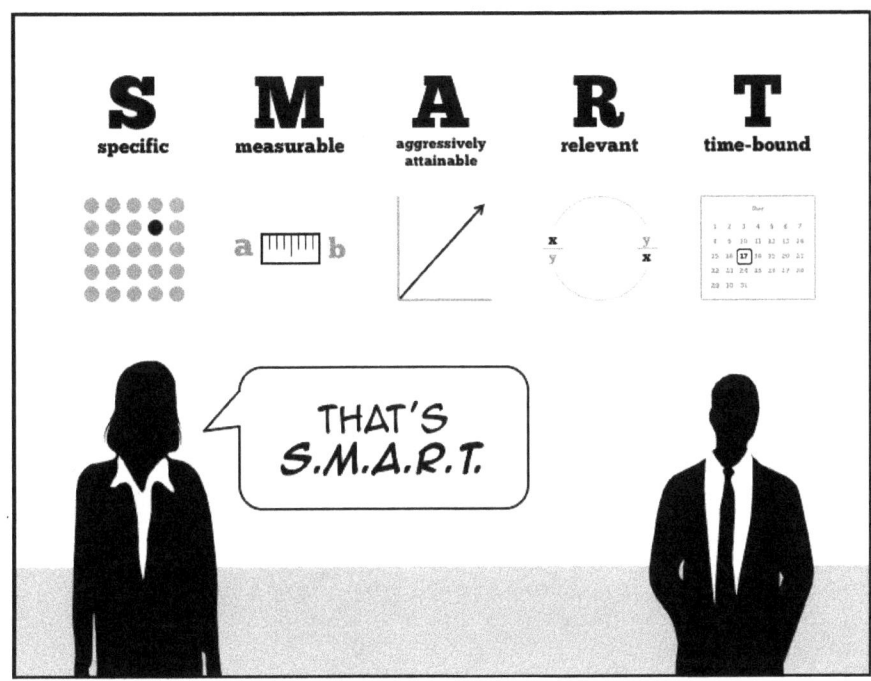

PART FOUR

MICKEY MEETS THE SMARTOMETER

SMARTometer Lite

		+/-	total
S	C01 – Is the action/decision/message/goal written down? — if yes, +50°	☐	☐
	C02 – Multiple goals/actions *(verbs, 'and', '.', or ',')*? — if yes, -30°	☐	☐
	C03 – Any ambiguous words? — if yes, -30°	☐	☐
M	C08 – Can we tell when we're done *(the 'to' or 'until')*? — if no, -30°	☐	☐
	C09 – Are 'robust' metrics in place? — if yes, +10°	☐	☐
A	C12 – Does it pass the 'Aggressively S.E.T.' test? — if yes, +10°	☐	☐
	C15 – Are there clear 'upside/downside' targets? — if yes, +10°	☐	☐
R	C16 – Does the 'why' matter *(mission, vision, values)*? — if no, -50°	☐	☐
	C19 – Any serious unintended consequences? — if yes, -20°	☐	☐
T	C23 – Is the date specified? — if yes, +10°	☐	☐
	C24 – Will this timeline 'win the race'? — if yes, +10°	☐	☐

Total ____

Stone Cold	Cold	Lukewarm	Warm	SMART as Hell
-120° ··· 0°	10° 20° 30°	40° 50° 60°	70° 80°	90° 100°

PERFECT.

HMMM... IN MY GOAL, 'TAKE CARE OF' IS *AMBIGUOUS*. I DON'T KNOW EXACTLY WHAT IT MEANS.

RIGHT. PHRASES LIKE 'TAKE CARE OF', 'SUPPORT', 'HELP', OR 'MANAGE' ARE WORSE THAN WORTHLESS.

THEY TRICK US INTO THINKING WE'RE ALIGNED WHEN WE'RE NOT.

DATA CONFIDENCE SCORECARD

	NEVER	ALMOST NEVER	SOMETIMES	ALMOST ALWAYS	ALWAYS
AVAILABILITY — IS THE DATA AVAILABLE TO YOU?	0	1	2	3	4
TIMELINESS — IS THE DATA TIMELY ENOUGH TO ACT UPON?	0	1	2	3	4
COMPLETENESS — IS THE DATA SET COMPLETE?	0	1	2	3	4
CLARITY — CAN YOU UNDERSTAND & EXPLAIN THE DATA?	0	1	2	3	4
RELIABILITY — CAN THE DATA SOURCE(S) BE VALIDATED?	0	1	2	3	4
CONSISTENCY — DO THE SAME INPUTS PRODUCE THE SAME OUTPUTS?	0	1	2	3	4
ACCURACY — DOES THE DATA ACCURATELY REFLECT REALITY?	0	1	2	3	4
BENCHMARKED — IS THE DATA BENCHMARKED AGAINST STANDARDS?	0	1	2	3	4

DATA CONFIDENCE: ____ / 32 = ____ %

DATA CONFIDENCE SCORECARD

	NEVER	ALMOST NEVER	SOMETIMES	ALMOST ALWAYS	ALWAYS
AVAILABILITY — IS THE DATA AVAILABLE TO YOU?		1			
TIMELINESS — IS THE DATA TIMELY ENOUGH TO ACT UPON?	0				
COMPLETENESS — IS THE DATA SET COMPLETE?		1			
CLARITY — CAN YOU UNDERSTAND & EXPLAIN THE DATA?			2		
RELIABILITY — CAN THE DATA SOURCE(S) BE VALIDATED?	?				
CONSISTENCY — DO THE SAME INPUTS PRODUCE THE SAME OUTPUTS?	?				
ACCURACY — DOES THE DATA ACCURATELY REFLECT REALITY?			2		
BENCHMARKED — IS THE DATA BENCHMARKED AGAINST STANDARDS?	0				

MICKEY'S SCORE: 6 / 24 =   25 %

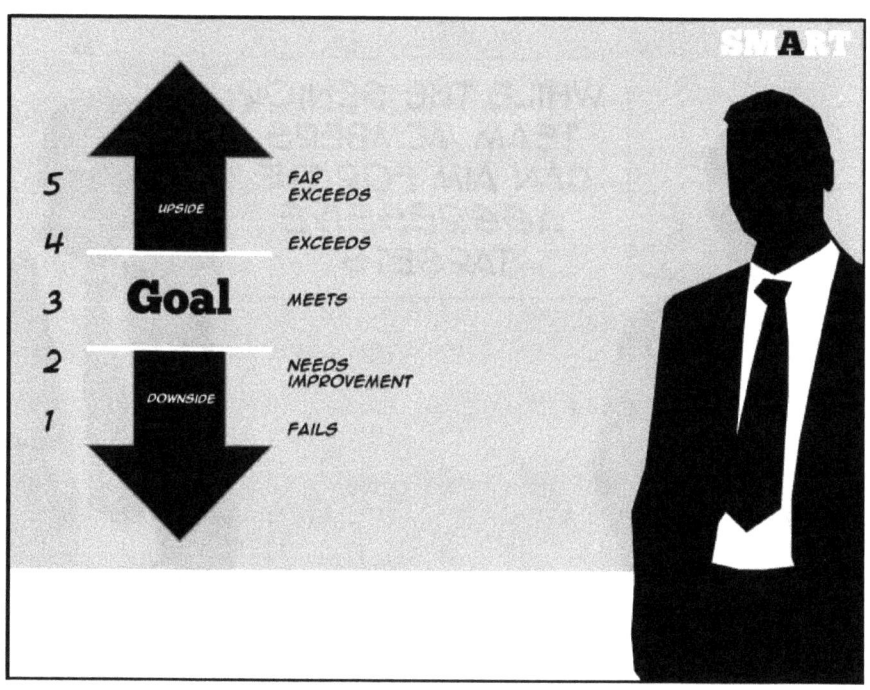

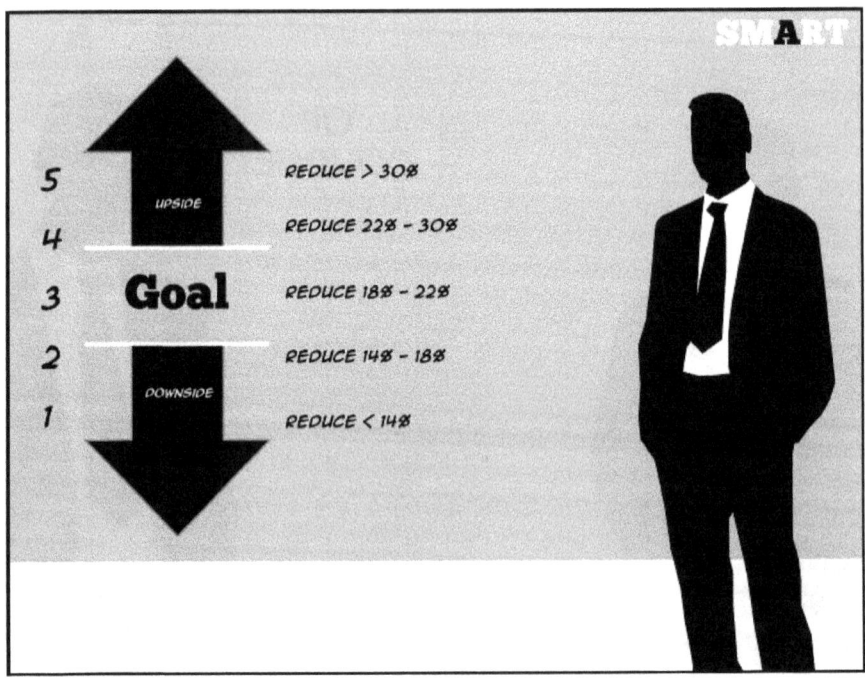

# SMA**R**T
Relevance is first among equals

> WE NEED TO MAKE SURE WE'RE WORKING ON THE RIGHT THINGS.

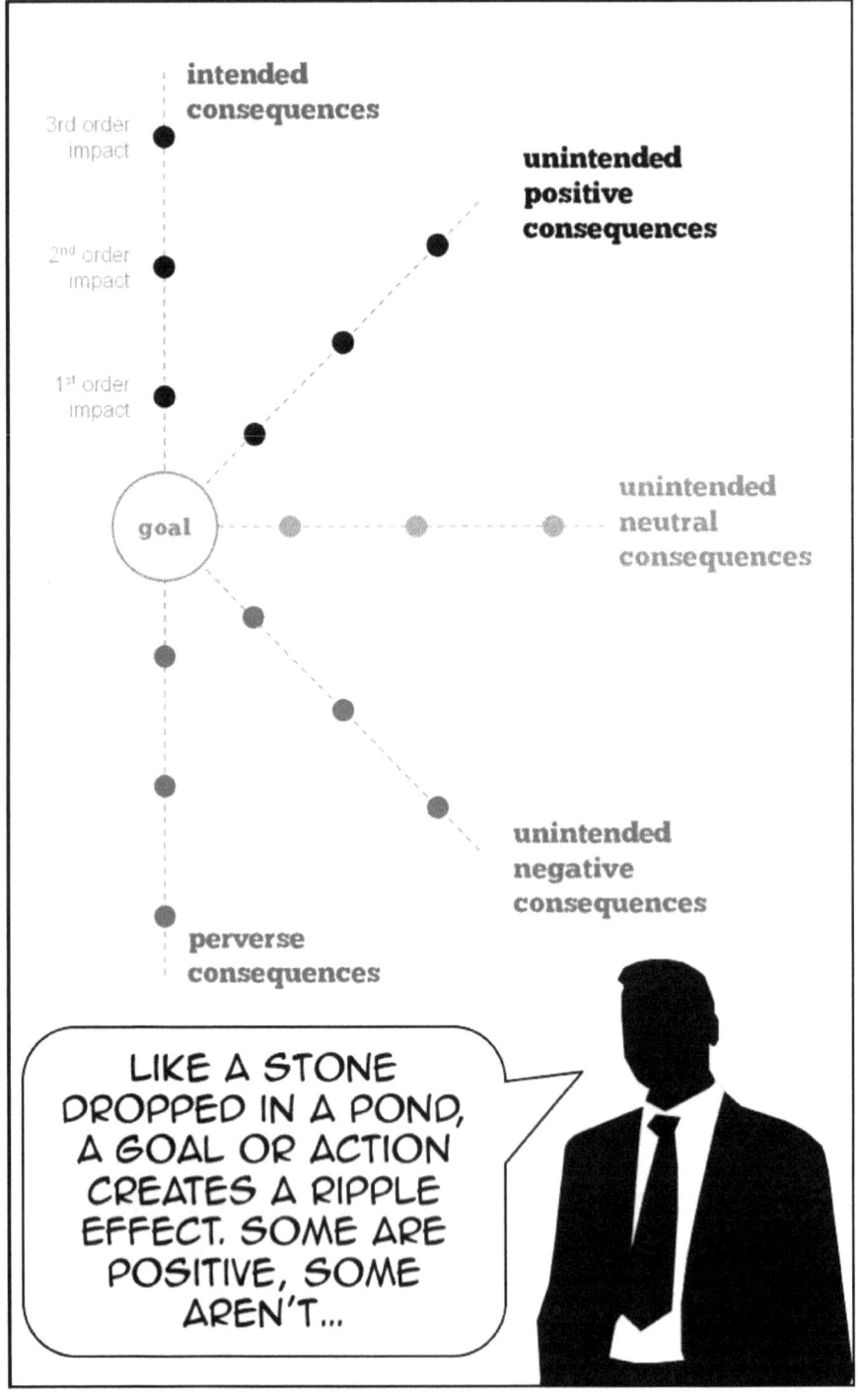

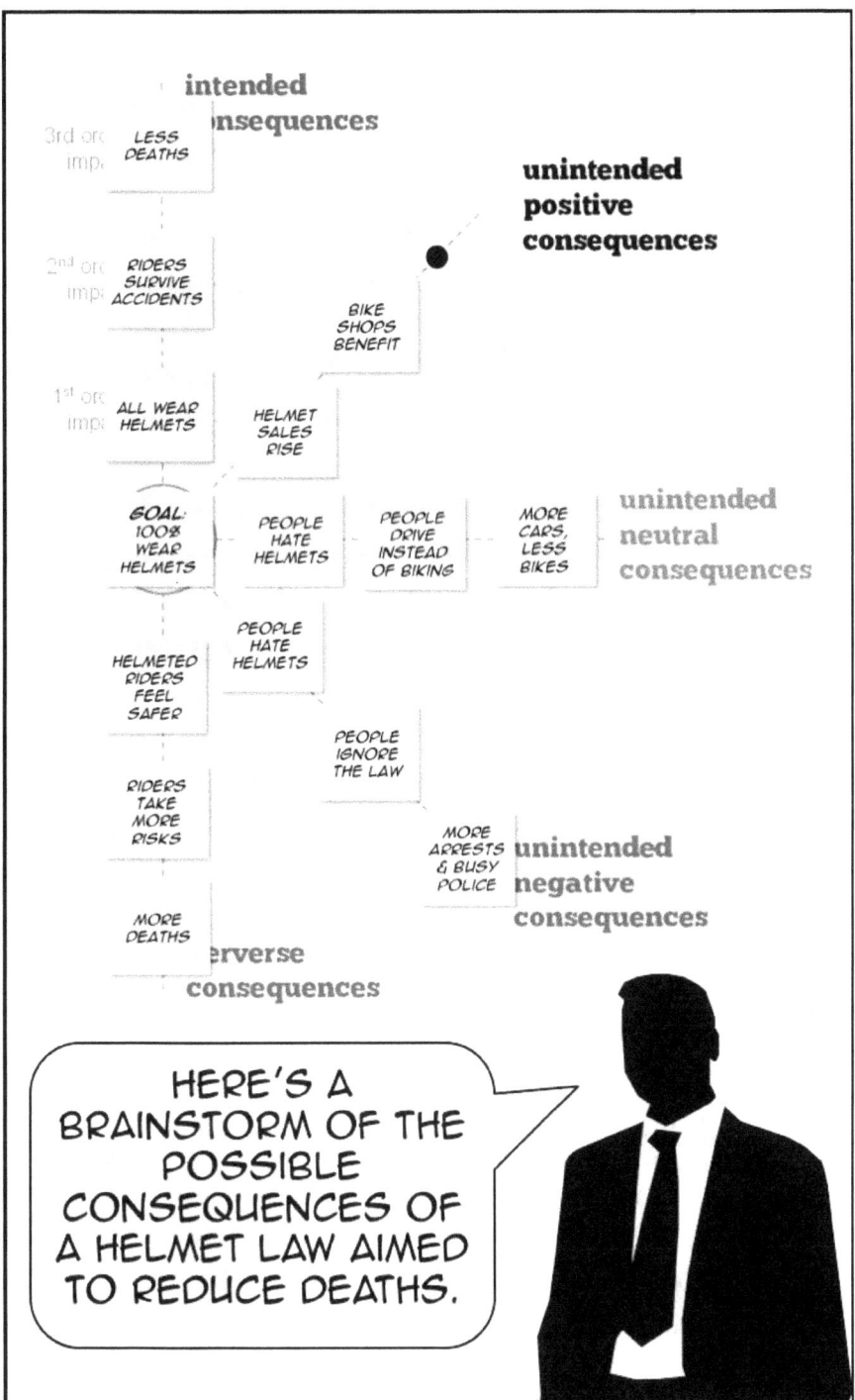

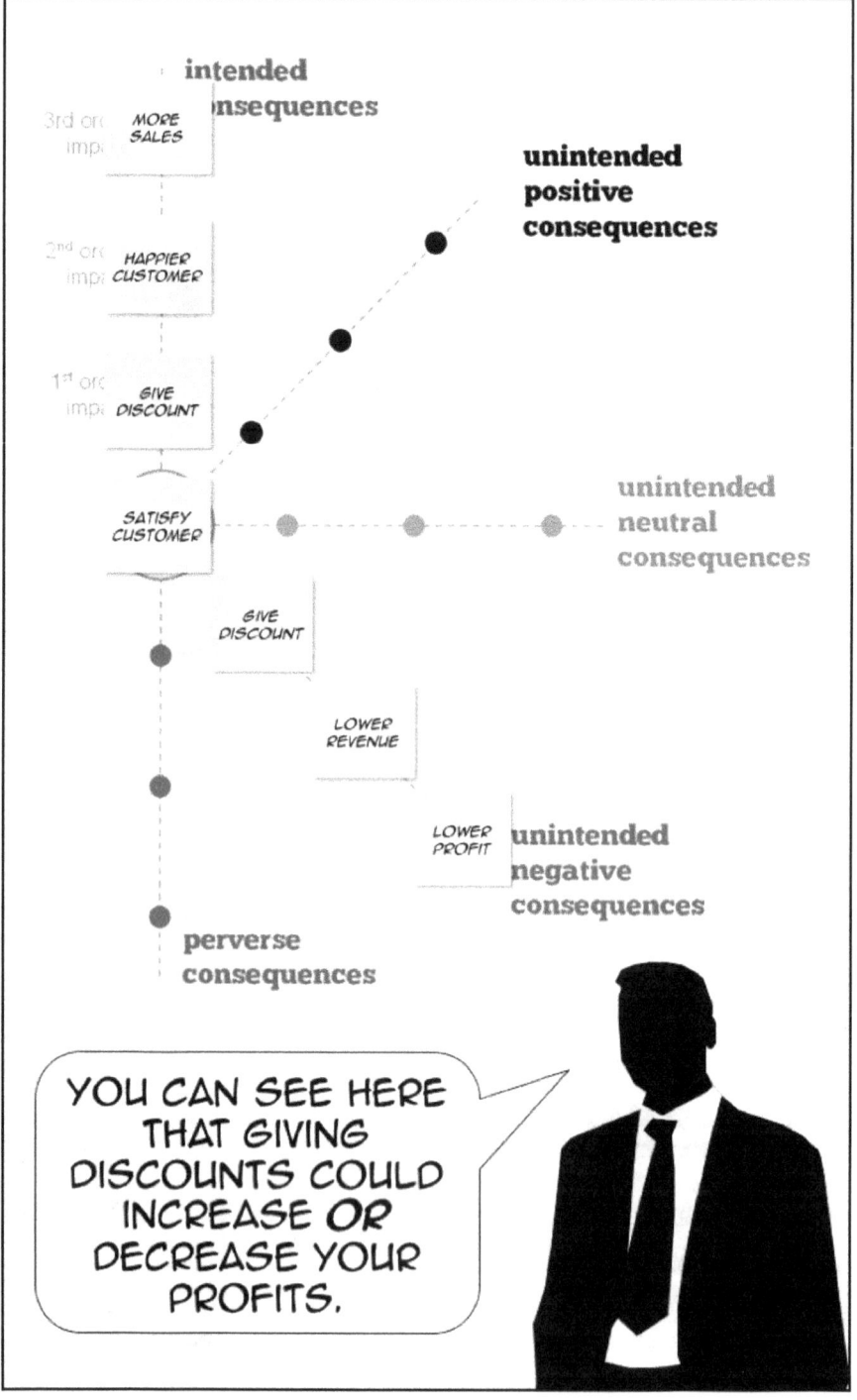

PART FIVE

MICKEY FINDS CLARITY

the SMARTsheet

Starting Goal:

R
- Why this goal?: _____
- If we don't, then: _____
- Counterproductive impact: _____

S
- Who: _____
- What: _____
- Where: _____

M
- Possible Measurements: _____
- Current Status ('From'): _____
- Target ('To'): _____
- What is 'Finished'?: _____

A
- Upside/Downside: _____
- More Aggressive?: _____

R
- Satisfy the 'Why?': _____
- Is it necessary?: _____
- Counterproductive Impact: _____

T
- Due Date? _____
- Other Milestones? _____
- 'Win the Race' Date? _____

the SMARTsheet

Starting Goal: IMPROVE CUSTOMER RELATIONSHIP

R
- Why this goal?: INCREASE SALES AND REVENUE
- If we don't, then: LOSE MARKET TO COMPETITION
- Counterproductive impact: NONE

S
- Who: KEY CUSTOMERS, TOP 10?
- What: SHARING OF KEY INFORMATION
- Where: CUSTOMER MEETINGS

M
- Possible Measurements: # OF CUSTOMERS
- Current Status ('From'): 3 OUT OF 10
- Target ('To'): 5 OR MORE OUT OF 10
- What is 'Finished'?: 10 OUT OF 10

A
- Upside/Downside: 6 OR 7 CUSTOMERS
- More Aggressive?: TRY FOR 8?

R
- Satisfy the 'Why?': YES
- Is it necessary?: YES, TO GET CLOSER
- Counterproductive Impact: TOO CLOSE TO CUSTOMER?

T
- Due Date?: MARCH 31ST
- Other Milestones?: TARGET ONE PER QUARTER
- 'Win the Race' Date?: TARGET ACME BY DEC 10TH

SMARTstoryboard

Who will do this? (name of person or group)	**WILL**	What will they do? (unambiguous verb) increase, improve, reduce, decrease, complete, release, submit, sustain, etc.
Modifier? (get specific)	What will they do? (unambiguous noun)	**WITH / FOR**
Who will this be done with or for?	**IN / AT / TO / ON**	Where will this be done? (place, location, product)
FROM	(starting point or baseline value)	**TO**
Finish point (target value with upside and downside)	**BY / ON**	(target date, time, or milestone)

WHAT WILL YOUR GOAL BE?

PART SIX

ALIGNMENT WITH AMY

SMARTstoryboard

I	WILL	INCREASE
TOP 10 CUSTOMERS	SHARING KEY INFORMATION	WITH / FOR
ME	IN / AT / TO / ON	CUSTOMER MEETINGS
FROM	THREE	TO
FIVE, WITH SIX BEING EXCEPTIONAL	BY / ON	MARCH 31ST OF THIS FISCAL YEAR

I USED THE SMARTSTORYBOARD AND CAME UP WITH THIS IDEA...

PART SEVEN

WRAPPING IT UP

PERSONAL	GRADUATE WITH AN MBA FROM STATE UNIVERSITY WITH A 3.5 GPA OR ABOVE WITHIN 3 YEARS.
HEALTH	REDUCE MY WEIGHT FROM 187 POUNDS TO 170 POUNDS BY JUNE 15TH.
FINANCIAL	INCREASE MY CREDIT SCORE FROM 590 TO 750 WITHIN 2 YEARS.
PROJECT	RECEIVE CUSTOMER SIGN-OFF ACCEPTING THE ALPHA PROJECT DESIGN BY DECEMBER 3RD.
PERFORMANCE REVIEWS	INCREASE SALES TO BETA ELECTRONICS BY 35% BY END OF THE SECOND QUARTER.
PRODUCTS	DESIGN AN AUTOMOBILE THAT TRAVELS 300 MILES ON A GALLON OF GAS BY 2020.
MEETINGS	SPEND 15 MINUTES TO REACH A 'GO/NO GO' DECISION ON THE PROPOSED SALES STRATEGY.
PRESENTATIONS	TODAY, I WOULD LIKE YOU TO APPROVE $10,000 FOR THE ALPHA PROJECT.
DELIVERABLES	RECRUITING WILL FORWARD 15 CANDIDATE RESUMES TO PATTY BY NOON, FRIDAY.
ACTION ITEMS	BOB WILL EMAIL THE VENDOR AGREEMENT TO SANDY BY THE END OF WEDNESDAY.
TRAINING	IN THIS TRAINING, YOU WILL REPLACE AN OIL FILTER CORRECTLY, IN 20 MINUTES OR LESS.
PROBLEM SOLVING	DECREASE LOST PACKAGE RATE FROM 2.1% TO 1.0% BY MAY 20TH.
MENTORING	I'D LIKE TO IDENTIFY 2 STRATEGIES FOR DEALING WITH MY DIFFICULT TEAMMATE.

SO HERE ARE THIRTEEN AREAS, WITH EXAMPLES, WHERE YOU CAN START WRITING *YOUR* GOALS.

WITH THIS BOOK, YOU'VE:

- ☐ DEFINED **SMART**
- ☐ MEASURED A GOAL WITH THE **SMARTOMETER LITE**
- ☐ BRAINSTORMED YOUR GOAL WITH THE **SMARTSHEET**
- ☐ WRITTEN A GOAL WITH THE **SMARTSTORYBOARD**, AND
- ☐ USED A NUMBER OF OTHER **SMART AS HELL** TOOLS

WHAT NOW?

- WRITE YOUR GOALS!
- VISIT **SMARTASHELL.COM**
- ATTEND SMART AS HELL LIVE!
- STAY IN TOUCH THROUGH:
  - TWITTER
  - PINTEREST
  - LINKEDIN

PART EIGHT

RESOURCES

MAKE THIS BOOK STRONGER!

This book is a living, evolving project. You're invited to co-create and co-design it in the following ways:

1. **DISTRIBUTED COPY-EDITING.** If you find typographical or conceptual errors, please let us know. We work with on-demand publishing technology that enables us to immediately incorporate your corrections and improvements.
2. **SHARE YOUR STORIES.** Send us the stories you have from your use of Smart as Hell Goals. Share big wins, horror stories, and small learning steps. If you're not sure how to tell your story, download the Seven Sentence Story Template from smartashell.com. We will collect and leverage your contributions in future editions.
3. **CONTRIBUTE TIPS.** Suggest additional pieces of advice based on your expertise and experience. We welcome your unusual and innovative ideas as well as traditional and tried-and-true ones.
4. **PROVIDE A REVIEW.** We love to get your unbiased reviews of our books on Amazon, barnesandnoble.com, or Goodreads.
5. **REQUEST ADDITIONAL FEATURES.** If there are general additions - chapters, graphics, tools, worksheets, videos - that you would like to see incorporated in future editions, let us know.

And remember, your easiest one-stop contact is *info@smartashell.com*

MORE, MORE, MORE!

WE'VE PROVIDED MULTIPLE WAYS TO CONTINUE YOUR SMART AS HELL EXPERIENCE:

- **WEBSITE**: SMARTASHELL.COM
- **EMAIL**: INFO@SMARTASHELL.COM
- **YOUTUBE**: YOUTUBE.COM/SMARTASHELLVIDEO
- **TWITTER**: TWITTER.COM/SMARTASHELL
- **LINKEDIN**: GLENN HUGHES
- **PINTEREST**: PINTEREST.COM/SMARTASHELL/
- **INSTAGRAM**: INSTAGRAM.COM/GLENN_HUGHES
- **AMAZON AUTHOR PAGE**: AMAZON.COM/AUTHOR/GHUGHES
- **GOODREADS**: GOODREADS.COM/GLENNHUGHES

- **SMART AS HELL WORKSHOPS & CERTIFICATION**: CONTACT US FOR LIVE OR VIRTUAL WORKSHOPS.
- **SMART AS HELL STYLE**: GET SHIRTS, MUGS, MOUSE PADS AND MORE AT ZAZZLE.COM/SMARTASHELL
- **PRINT SHOP**: CREATE SMART AS HELL GOALS WITH POSTERS, WORKSHEETS, AND PLANNERS AVAILABLE AT MARKETPLACE.MIMEO.COM/SMART
- **BOOKS**: FIND ALL OF THE BOOKS IN THE SMART AS HELL SERIES AT SMARTASHELL.COM OR AMAZON.COM.

ABOUT THE AUTHOR

GLENN HUGHES IS AN AWARD-WINNING AUTHOR, PHOTOGRAPHER, FACILITATOR, AND LEARNING LEADER.

GLENN IS SENIOR DIRECTOR OF LEARNING AND DEVELOPMENT AT KLA-TENCOR CORPORATION. KLA-TENCOR'S LEARNING ORGANIZATION WAS RECOGNIZED IN 2008 AS A CHARTER MEMBER OF TRAINING MAGAZINE'S *"TRAINING TOP 10 HALL OF FAME"* AFTER PLACING IN THE WORLD'S TOP 10 TRAINING ORGANIZATIONS FOR 5 CONSECUTIVE YEARS.

GLENN IS ALSO THE FOUNDER OF *SMART AS HELL*, A COMPANY THAT HELPS INDIVIDUALS AND ORGANIZATIONS CHANGE THEIR WORLD ONE GOAL AT A TIME. SMART AS HELL DEVELOPS BEST PRACTICES IN GOAL WRITING AND ACHIEVEMENT - INCLUDING THE GROUNDBREAKING *SMARTOMETER*, A TOOL FOR MEASURING THE EFFECTIVENESS OF GOALS.

GLENN'S FIRST BOOK, *"PHOTO JOLTS! IMAGE-BASED ACTIVITIES THAT INSPIRE CLARITY, CREATIVITY, AND CONVERSATION"* WAS CO-WRITTEN WITH INTERACTIVE LEARNING GURU SIVASAILAM 'THIAGI' THIAGARAJAN. *"PHOTO JOLTS!"* RECEIVED THE ISPI (INTERNATIONAL SOCIETY FOR PERFORMANCE IMPROVEMENT) 2014 AWARD OF EXCELLENCE FOR OUTSTANDING HUMAN PERFORMANCE COMMUNICATION.

GLENN HAS RECEIVED FIVE FACILITATION IMPACT AWARDS FROM THE INTERNATIONAL ASSOCIATION OF FACILITATORS, RECOGNIZING THE WORLD-CLASS RESULTS THAT HE AND HIS CLIENTS HAVE ACHIEVED.

HE IS A FREQUENT SPEAKER AT INTERNATIONAL CONFERENCES SUCH AS ATD (THE ASSOCIATION FOR TALENT DEVELOPMENT), ISPI (THE INTERNATIONAL SOCIETY FOR PERFORMANCE IMPROVEMENT), LAKEWOOD'S TRAINING CONFERENCES, AND THE IAF (INTERNATIONAL ASSOCIATION OF FACILITATORS).

GLENN LIVED IN ASIA FOR MORE THAN 10 YEARS, WORKING WITH MANY OF THE WORLD'S LARGEST ELECTRONICS COMPANIES WHILE MANAGING MULTI-MILLION DOLLAR OPERATIONS IN CHINA, SINGAPORE, AND JAPAN. HE HOLDS A MASTER'S DEGREE IN ADULT EDUCATION AND TRAINING AND A BACHELOR'S DEGREE IN ELECTRONICS ENGINEERING TECHNOLOGY.

THE SMART AS HELL LIBRARY

PHOTO JOLTS! IMAGE-BASED ACTIVITIES THAT INCREASE CLARITY, CREATIVITY, AND CONVERSATION
BY GLENN HUGHES & SIVASAILAM 'THIAGI' THIAGARAGAN
FOREWORD BY NANCY DUARTE
$29.99, SUMMER 2013

A GRAPHIC GUIDE TO WRITING SMART AS HELL GOALS
FOREWORD BY SIVASAILAM 'THIAGI' THIAGARAJAN
$24.99, FALL 2015

SMART AS HELL ADVICE: A YEAR'S WORTH OF WISDOM FOR GOAL ACHIEVEMENT AND SUCCESS
FOREWORD BY BRENT BLOOM
$14.99, FALL 2015

THE SMART AS HELL SESSIONS: FOUR CONVERSATIONS ON THE ART OF CREATING SMART GOALS THAT WORK
FOREWORD BY CAL WICK
$24.99, WINTER 2015

SMART AS HELL: A MANIFESTO FOR ACTION, ALIGNMENT, AND ACHIEVEMENT
$29.99, SPRING 2016

THE RUBRICS REVOLUTION: 200 SCORECARDS FOR IMPROVING PERSONAL AND PROFESSIONAL PERFORMANCE
$24.99, SPRING 2016

MOVVERRS: HOW YOUR SMART AS HELL MISSION, VISION, VALUES, ROLES & RESPONSIBILITIES, AND STRATEGIES DRIVE ENERGY, ENGAGEMENT, AND EXECUTION
FOREWORD BY ED MUZIO
$24.99, SUMMER 2016

THE SMART AS HELL NOTEBOOKS: A RIGHT-BRAIN GUIDE TO GOAL-SETTING
$19.99, FALL 2016

CONTACT GLENN:

CONTACT GLENN HUGHES AT:
- SMARTASHELL.COM
- INFO@SMARTASHELL.COM

FIND SUPPLEMENTAL VIDEOS, WORKSHEETS, AND LINKS AT:

HTTP://SMARTASHELL.COM/BLOG/SAHGG

www.ingramcontent.com/pod-product-compliance
Lightning Source LLC
Chambersburg PA
CBHW070643160426
43194CB00009B/1558